A Memoir By Rev. Carlos Leiva

FROM THE HOUSE OF TERROR

To The House of Light

Call to Me, and I will answer you,
and show you great and mighty
things, which you do not know.

Jeremiah 33:3, NKJV

FROM THE HOUSE OF TERROR TO THE HOUSE OF LIGHT

A Young Boy's Remarkable Journey from Trauma to Triumph

A Memoir

By Rev. Carlos Leiva

Into The Light Ministry
Silver Spring, MD

Published 2025 by Into The Light Ministry, Silver Spring, MD

From The House of Terror To The House of Light:
A Young Boy's Remarkable Journey From Trauma to Triumph

A Memoir by Rev. Carlos Leiva

ISBN (paperback): 979-8-218-71419-2
Library of Congress Control Number: 2025912771

Cover design and interior layout
by Eddie Egesi, 2025

I dedicate this book to my beloved wife, Wendy, for all the love, patience, care, and resilience that she endured through my sickness and trials.

CONTENTS

INTRODUCTION

This memoir is a true story of my upbringing in a home that stood in contrast to the character God desires to instill in each of us. It tells the story of many hardships I endured, beginning at the early age of seven and continuing into adulthood. These struggles drove me to seek misguided, temporary relief through drug use, which eventually led to addiction. Caught in the grip of that addiction, I was drawn into making poor choices that pulled me even further away from God.

The further I walked away from God—and from being a healthy, stable person—the more difficult and depressing life became. Life turned into a daily nightmare instead of a walk of victorious living. Things continued to worsen, and each day became harder to bear than the one before. There are parts of this book that were very difficult to write because of how personal and haunting they are.

The purpose of this book is not to seek pity, but to show people that they can overcome any obstacle or tragedy they may face. I have endured what feels like ten lifetimes of suffering, and I just want you to know that no matter how difficult your problem is, there are real solutions outlined through this book.

The Good News!

I believe that anyone who follows the simple instructions in this book can be liberated from any trauma, sickness, or depression. Every piece of advice I share comes from what I've lived and practiced myself. I am living proof that there are real, proven steps a person can take to overcome any trauma, addiction, and illness.

So come—take a walk with me through these pages, as I lead you out of the sicknesses and torments that have temporarily bound and afflicted you.

CHAPTER 1

Where it all began

My life started in a medium sized, clean, wooded, middle-class neighborhood in Silver Spring Maryland. The neighborhood I grew up in was called Woodmoor; because of the vast number of trees which accented the landscape and rolling hills.

Before I continue, I want to tell you a little bit about my mother. My mother was a very loving woman. She was nice to most of my friends—except for the bad ones. You should know better than to try to fool any mother, especially mine. She was a hard-working person with an extraordinarily strong character. If she liked somebody, she would treat them like angels. If she didn't like someone, she would make it known through her facial expressions and tone of voice. In her mind, there was no middle ground—you were either an angel of God or a child of the devil.

She suffered from a combination of depression and schizophrenia. These two illnesses together affected her moods and personality. One moment, she could be laughing and cheerful;

the next, she would grow quiet, serious, or angry. Depression is a terrible burden on its own, but when paired with schizophrenia, it becomes even more difficult. The schizophrenic side made her extremely suspicious and paranoid. Sadly, my poor mom was born this way.

Screams of Horror

I was in elementary school, in the third grade. This is where the real-life drama, my horror story—began.

One evening, I was walking home from playing basketball at school with a group of friends. The closer we got to my house, the louder we could hear my mom screaming at the top of her lungs, "I want to die," repeatedly. Hearing this always crushed my heart, as you can imagine. I wished I were an angel so I could fly away into the clouds. Words like "horrible" and "depressed" don't even come close to describing how I felt.

One person in the group I was playing basketball with asked me, "Was that your mom I just heard yelling?" I sadly lowered my head in shame and replied, "Yes." It was too obvious to deny that something was wrong. I felt like I wanted to disappear off the face of the earth in that moment. My friends continued to ask what was wrong with my mother. I replied, "She gets sick some-times and goes into these yelling fits." They had blank looks on their faces and said, "We are sorry to hear about this."

The next day at school, the people I thought were my friends had told one of the gossiping students that my mother was crazy. This betrayal hit me like a ton of bricks. From that day on, the bullies would come up to me and say, "I heard your mother is crazy!" This put me in a very awkward situation. On top of hearing my mother yell that she wants to die—because she was suffering from severe depression—I now had to deal with bullies making fun of her. How would you feel if you were in this situation? It caused me a lot of pain and trauma as a third grader.

These outbursts occurred about once every two weeks. When they happened, my dad would rush into the bedroom to try to comfort her. I would run out of my room and into my parents' room, where she would be lying on the bed, clenching her fists and yelling, "I want to die," repeatedly, as loud as she could.

My mother would thrash around on the bed in agony when these attacks occurred. My dad would take her hand and say, "It's okay. You're going to be all right." When I asked him what was wrong with my mother, he would downplay the episode and say, "Oh, she just doesn't feel well."

It was painfully obvious that something was seriously wrong with her. My dad tried to downplay her illness so that his two sons wouldn't suffer more trauma than they already had. I remember watching my dad's face grow paler after each outburst. I remember asking God to please heal my mother.

After 15 minutes or so, my mother would begin to calm down, and her breathing would return to normal. I would hug her and tell her that I loved her. This went on for eight years.

Thankfully, after several long years, her outbursts of depression and anxiety finally diminished. I was so relieved when I no longer heard my mom in agony. The painful, soul-crushing screaming had stopped. We were all thrilled by the progress she made in overcoming those panic-driven, depressive, and at times—demonic attacks. We were overjoyed.

Looking back, I realize that God and my dad were the only two who comforted me during those difficult times. I knew God existed—I just didn't know how to find Him. I am beyond thankful that God healed my mother.

A little about my mother's character

My mother was the disciplinarian in the house. When the kids needed to be disciplined, she had no problem doing so.

Unfortunately, she would backhand my brother and me in the face as a method of discipline. This was highly inappropriate and is now recognized as an abusive way to discipline children. In this day and age, it is considered child abuse—and there are thousands of kids living in similar situations.

My mother would over-discipline me for the smallest things. I remember laughing at something I thought was funny, but she did not find it amusing and lost her temper. She would haul off and backhand me in the face with her big knuckles—sometimes with large semi-precious stones on her fingers. This abusive behavior made it exceedingly difficult for a child to bond with or even get close to a parent.

Every time she smacked me in the face, I felt depressed and worthless. This abuse deeply affected my self-esteem.

As time went on, fast-forwarding to the age of 15, my mother pulled me aside, sat me down at the kitchen table, and said, "Did you know that your dad and I didn't plan to have you?" My face flushed, and my emotions froze as I entered yet another moment of traumatic emotional paralysis.

I could have gone my whole life without hearing that I was an unplanned child. To this day, I still don't understand why she chose to reveal this to me. Knowing that I was unplanned made me feel even more rejected and unloved than I already felt.

If a child knows that he or she was not planned, it can make them feel insecure, unloved, rejected, and confused.

If you are a parent, I implore you—please never tell your child that they were not planned. There is no positive outcome to sharing that information. It damages the child's psychological and spiritual growth. It can lead to depression, trauma, rejection, and low self-esteem—especially if the parent also struggles with anger issues.

If you hit your child in the face or with objects, you are committing a crime called child abuse. Please repent from this abusive act, even if you believe it to be discipline or punishment. Just because your parents may have disciplined you this way does not make it right. It is not discipline; it is physical abuse and should be reported to someone outside of the family—a mature adult or a Christian counselor.

To those who are victims of abuse: If the abuse is severe and ongoing, consider speaking with a trusted adult outside of your home and reporting it to the proper authorities. If I had not been so terrified as a child, calling the proper authorities would have been a wise and necessary step to stop the abuse. It's a decision that any victim has the right to consider.

The reason a lot of young children do not report physical abuse

Some children know that if you report something like this to the police, protective services can sometimes take the child into their custody. This is the very reason I never reported the abuse I was experiencing—not just from my mother, but from my brother as well. I was afraid of being taken to a government-run foster home. I had heard other kids talk about abuse at those facilities, and it would occasionally come up in the news.

I confided in a friend about my abusive household. He sat there silently for a few moments, contemplating the situation. He said, "Carlos, this is serious. If you report this to the authorities, I guarantee you that the government will come and remove you from your home." I was already scared of people in general, and I didn't have the courage to face an even worse situation.

"Then they'll put you in a government-run foster facility," he continued, explaining that he had heard horror stories about children being abused by caretakers in those places.

At that point, I felt trapped. I didn't want to end up in a foster care facility, where I might be treated even worse than I was at home. So, I chose to stay at home and endure the abuse until the age of 17.

I tried to defend myself from the abuse.

At the age of 13, I grabbed my mother's hands as she was about to smack me in the face. By that point, I had more than enough of the abuse. I said to her, "Don't ever hit me in the face again," and I put her hands down by her side.

She started acting like a frightened victim and told my older brother—who was 12 years older than me—about the situation. He told me never to do that again or I would be in big trouble.

I was terrified of my brother. You'll learn more about him and why I feared him in the following chapters.

I could hardly wait to turn 17 so I could move out of that house of hell, pain, torment, and depression.

There are better, healthier ways to discipline a child. Smacking them in the face is not the way a child should be corrected. Instead, try taking away privileges like going outside, playing, or watching TV.

You can also take away their computer or phone, if they have one. A child can understand these types of consequences and will learn from them. They are more likely to grow into strong and mentally healthy young adults. Years later, I met a friend whose parents never hit him. He was highly intelligent, emotionally balanced, and healthy. Knowing how to correctly discipline your children is crucial to ensuring they grow up to be mentally and emotionally stable. Those spirits of anger and abuse can be passed on to them as they get older.

A side note to all parents

If you are abusively raising your children by slapping them in the face, you are destroying their emotional, psychological, and spiritual growth. You are also causing severe inferiority, low self-esteem, anxiety, depression, and—worst of all—fear. If you are disciplining your child in this way, it likely means you have unresolved anger issues and need counseling from a mental health professional. You should also consider seeking spiritual help from a pastor who practices deliverance. These harmful spiritual influences must be confronted and cast out, in Jesus' name.

You can be properly instructed on how to discipline and communicate with your child. Speaking with a professional Christian counselor and reading Christian resources on healthy discipline can be very educational and will guide you toward a more positive outcome. No good parent wants to see their child mentally scarred and traumatized.

These are some unfortunate repercussions of abusive parenting.

The list of repercussions would take up too many pages to include in this book. So, I will begin by discussing a few major problems associated with being slapped in the face as a form of discipline.

One of the first issues abuse causes in a child is low self-esteem. When a child is slapped in the face, they feel as if they've done something terribly wrong. They immediately begin to experience feelings of guilt, worthlessness, anxiety, shame, low self-confidence, depression, and rejection. I personally lived through this—so I know this is what happens.

The victim feels worthless, hated, and unwanted. Guilt and false guilt are also common emotions that arise after being slapped in the face.

This is only the beginning of the effects of being hit in the face. These traumas may cause a child to seek quick—but destructive—forms of relief, such as drugs and other addictions.

I lived through this experience and initially chose the wrong solution. I almost left out two especially important emotions: resentment and bitterness toward the abuser. These feelings often lead the victim into rebellion.

Physical abuse also creates a lack of respect for authority. If you're a parent wondering why your child is rebellious, consider that it may stem from your own uncontrolled anger and lack of parenting skills. If you truly love your child, please seek the proper help and repent of this behavior. If you don't, you're allowing the devil to use you to destroy your sons and daughters.

Feeling rejected and finding a proper solution.

An abused child will often choose to associate with others who have similar problems. This makes them vulnerable, and they may cling to people who have also been abused, traumatized, depressed, or addicted to drugs. The victim finds common ground with other abused kids, which makes them feel accepted. That sense of shared experience becomes the spark that ignites a search for quick and simple solutions.

A hurting person seeks immediate relief from the pain, anxiety, and depression that abuse causes. In the beginning, it can feel helpful to talk with people who can relate to similar problems. The victim may find temporary comfort in sharing their experiences with others.

But the danger is that this often becomes a self-destructive cycle. You can only talk about problems for so long before it leads to a downward spiral of desperation and depression.

An educated, decisive action must be taken quickly—before the child turns to destructive solutions like drug use. Acting swiftly to get experienced psychological and spiritual counseling can provide the urgent help a child needs—and may very well save their life.

The problem with most people I met when I was younger was that instead of seeking a counselor or a pastor to help guide them through their situation, they turned to drugs, crime, and fornication to satisfy and alleviate their pain.

An abused child will try anything out of desperation to relieve the pain and trauma they are experiencing. The pain does not simply go away on its own. If the adolescent does not seek proper help for gradual healing, these afflictions may lead them to find other ways to numb their pain and depression. Unfortunately, many turn to drugs.

Most abused kids are afraid to come forward because of shame, fear, rejection, not being believed, or the risk of being punished more severely by the abuser.

I hesitated to include this, but the victim can become so tormented that they may lash out at the abuser with lethal force.

I saw a news program years ago about a teenage boy who was beaten by his father. The mother and younger brother were also victims of the abuse. One day, the boy found his dad's rifle and took revenge. He is now facing fifty years to life in prison for his actions.

This is a tragic ending to four lives. Abuse is not something to be taken lightly. It must be dealt with through both physical and spiritual counseling. The spirits of trauma and anger must be cast out by a minister or a devout believer in Jesus.

Counseling

Some kids feel that going to see a counselor means they are crazy or that something is severely wrong with them. This causes them to feel separated from the so-called "normal," balanced kids who were not abused.

The idea that a child must see a counselor can make them feel anxious, worried, depressed, and afraid. It causes them to feel different from other kids. This can lead to a life of isolation, feelings of inferiority, and depression.

It's important to seek a God-fearing Christian counselor who can lovingly explain to the child that what they are doing is completely normal and wise. The counselor must also emphasize that there is nothing to be ashamed of.

I am a mature adult now and I know that the right type of Godly counseling—and being part of a Christian, Bible-teaching church—can help a child recover from the symptoms and scars of abuse. The person who needs healing must first ask God to cleanse them from all sin, and then invite Jesus into his or her heart. Jesus is the healer, and He was the primary one who healed me. Other methods, including good counseling, were secondary in my personal recovery from abuse. Psychology is a helpful guide that encourages personal action and responsibility, along with medication. But this is only part of the solution.

I was not truly whole until two ministers and a pastor prayed and bound the spirits of alcoholism and depression that had run in my family for generations. It wasn't until after that prayer that I felt truly free from those evil spirits. I stood up from the floor with the minister's help, and it felt as though a million pounds had been lifted from my soul and body. Jesus gave me the privilege of witnessing those spirits leave my physical body, one after another.

I didn't tell the ministers that I saw the demons leave because it felt too personal and honestly, a little embarrassing. But I did tell them that I felt a huge weight lifted from me—and I believe they saw it too before I hit the ground.

A child might think it's the end of the world to seek counseling. But the truth is quite the opposite. Seeing a counselor—or a Christian psychologist—can help you heal, forgive, grow spiritually, and find victory over this extremely serious struggle.

Counseling helps children deal with the traumatic pain they are feeling. They will learn coping mechanisms and be guided through the steps necessary for healing. I strongly recommend that the child be rooted in a Bible-believing Christian church— one that practices deliverance and teaches the Word of God. Look for a church with an experienced pastor and a proven record of helping abused people and casting out spirits of trauma, depression, and premature death.

I write all of this from personal experience and a place of complete healing. Today, I am healed from alcoholism, trauma, and depression. I believe a mechanic cannot fix a complex electrical problem with book knowledge alone. His hands-on experience with electrical wiring makes his understanding far more useful. In the same way, my healing experience gives me the ability to teach and testify with authority.

I could go on and on about the damage that child abuse causes. It truly feels like living in a horror movie. The damage is real— and if not addressed quickly and properly, it can lead to drug addiction and even death.

These are the steps I took to heal the wounds, trauma, and depression I experienced.

CHAPTER 2

The Move to Philadelphia, Shadowed by Illness

My mother drank alcohol daily, and the fact that she did not even know she was pregnant until months later caused me to be born with small fiber neuropathy(SFN) and depression.

Explanation of Small fiber neuropathy

Small fiber neuropathy is a nerve condition that leads to severe pain attacks. It feels like someone is sticking you with a pin all over your body at different intervals—and continuously. It's a horrible sensation that causes intense anxiety and stress.

Imagine someone pricking your right arm with a pin, then two seconds later your left leg, and then behind your neck. It's a constant cycle that never ends, day or night. This pain made it exceedingly difficult for me to memorize things I needed to study, both in school and life in general. My mind was so tormented by the constant pain that I also found it difficult to concentrate.

Depression also makes it hard to carry out the responsibilities of daily life. It steals your motivation and drains your energy.

My mom's daily drinking habit did not help her depression or schizophrenia. She was what they would call a functioning alcoholic—someone who relies on alcohol to get through the day. This can be especially dangerous during pregnancy, as it can lead to birth defects or developmental issues in a child.

I explained to my mother that I felt pins and needles poking me all over my body. She replied to me saying, "I feel them too sometimes; but we all feel pain—be strong, it's okay." I took her misguided advice and tolerated the pain for years. I tried to self-medicate and sought counselling, but the pain was never resolved.

There are different kinds of pain, but physical pain should always be investigated and treated by a physician. Doctors are here to help us. Their knowledge, gained through years of study, can be an immense help to humanity.

Twenty-five years later, in the year 2007, the neuropathic pain became so intense that I could no longer block it out. It completely drained my energy to zero. That was when I finally sought medical help.

I was accurately diagnosed in 2007, with tests confirming that I had small fiber neuropathy. This made studying, sitting, memorizing, and concentrating for extended periods exceedingly difficult. It affected my schoolwork, daily life, and my ability to grow and excel at a steady rate—like everyone else. Most of my energy was

14

being drained by the physical pain caused by the neuropathy, along with the depression I felt.

Depression is often linked to low levels of serotonin and nor-epinephrine in the brain. It affects your concentration, energy levels, and overall ability to function as efficiently as others. It can also make you feel isolated or different from those around you, leading to negative thinking, low self-esteem, and feelings of inferiority.

Catholic school in Philadelphia and more abuse.

My parents moved us to Philadelphia when I was in the third grade, seeking a better and more prosperous life. My mother often talked about being able to afford a private school for my brother and me. They had great ambitions and an excellent plan for prosperity. At one point, my parents even opened a Spanish restaurant with another couple they knew.

My grandmother moved in with us for a few months at the beginning of our stay in Philadelphia. Unfortunately, during this period, my parents' relationship was unstable. They argued frequently, and the loud fights made everyone—especially my grandmother—extremely uncomfortable.

After a short while, my grandmother left Philadelphia and returned to her home in Paris, France. This made me incredibly sad because she truly loved me and treated me like no one else had. She never hit me in the face, and always showed me love and care. If you show and give someone love, they naturally reciprocate that feeling. If a parent snaps at a child with yelling or physical abuse, the child is left traumatized—feeling rejected, which can lead to low self-esteem, oversensitivity, anxiety, and depression.

My parents worked hard for long hours and would sometimes not come home until 1:30 to 2am in the morning. While they were at work, my brother oversaw and took care of me.

I attended St. Charles Catholic school in Philadelphia. In the third grade, the nuns were our teachers and had the right to physically hit us, as a form of discipline. This so-called discipline was often severe.

My parents' dream of sending me to a private Catholic school came true —but for me, their dream became a nightmare I had to endure and, eventually, overcome.

To this day, I am completely against that kind of discipline. In fact, it is not discipline—it is child abuse. You will see why in the following paragraphs.

In the 1970s, certain private schools were given the authority to physically discipline children. This, in my opinion, was very wrong.

I remember a couple of occasions when I did not finish my homework on time; the nun would come to my desk and command me to lay both of my hands flat on it. Then she would take a wooden ruler and slap the back of my hands extremely hard. I would begin to cry, but this didn't faze the nuns at all. They were very cold, mean, and callous. Their actions instilled fear—not the respectful kind, but a fear so intense that it made children shake, tremble, and cry.

On another occasion, when I again failed to finish my homework, a nun called me to stand in front of the class. I will never forget what happened next. She grabbed me by the ears and pushed on my skull with both hands, then lifted me about three feet off the ground in front of the entire class. I had never experienced such pain or embarrassment in my life until that day. I cried aloud as it happened. There was absolutely no remorse, no compassion, no care in their actions. The nuns operated like military drill sergeants—except they were sanctioned to inflict physical pain on children. What I experienced was enough to traumatize even the strongest child.

The neuropathy and depression drained me both physically and mentally. This made it difficult to complete all the assignments that I was given in class. It also caused me to fall behind on homework.

I remember how desperately I wanted to get out of that school. I absolutely hated how the nuns were able to get away with that kind of abuse. Today, those actions would be recognized as child abuse and would not be tolerated or legal in any school or institution.

More abuse at home

One afternoon after school, I was exhausted and fell asleep with my head resting on my hands at my desk.

I woke up to my brother—who is 12 years older than me—yelling at me and violently shaking my arm, telling me to wake up. He shouted, "Do your homework, now!"

I asked him if I could please continue my nap because I was very tired. I promised him I would do my homework a little later, after a short rest. I needed naps to regain the energy that my illnesses and abuse had drained from me.

My brother yelled out again, "Do your homework now!"

He then removed his belt and started lashing me from the top of my head to my feet. I cried and begged him to please stop, but it did no good. He continued to beat me all over my body with his belt, as hard as he could.

He whipped me for at least 10 minutes, until my body was covered in scars. When he saw the marks, he looked frighted. He told me not to tell our mother, or I'd get it worse next time. He told me to only wear long-sleeved shirts and long pants until the scars healed.

I went to school for the next month wearing long sleeves and long pants to cover up the bruises all over my body. I cannot fully describe the fear that filled my heart—a deep, traumatizing fear.

I wondered how my mother did not notice the scars. I believe she did notice, but stayed silent out of fear that the police might find out. If they had, then my brother would have gone to jail.

He was not a minor when this incident happened, he was 19 years old, already an adult. My mother was very protective of my brother and would do anything in her power to protect him.

In my mother's defense, she suffered from depression and schizophrenia. These two diseases hampered her ability to make good decisions. She must have seen the scars and yelled at him—at least once.

Still, this does not excuse a parent favoring one child over another. It is a cynical, careless, and selfish act. Any parent who does this should be ashamed and repent. Favoritism causes emotional damage and delays both the psychological and spiritual growth of the less-favored child.

Chapter 2

A note to all parents who have favorite kids

If you show favor to one of your children, please do not be naïve in thinking that the other—who is less favored—does not notice.

The less favored child notices every action, emotion, and detail you display toward the one you favor. This affects the child deeply, often making them oversensitive to correction and discipline. Favoritism also leads to low self-esteem, low self-confidence, feelings of rejection, and depression.

It causes even more damage than most realize, but these are just a few of the major symptoms experienced by the least favored child.

If you want to be a good parent, you must change this cynical, selfish behavior and stop the favoritism. God loves all of His children equally and does not shame any of them by showing more love to one than another.

The Spanish restaurant and the family's downfall.

Earlier, I mentioned that my mom and dad started a Spanish restaurant in Philadelphia with another couple. The other couple owned half of the restaurant, and my parents owned the other half.

The restaurant was doing great. I remember my dad counting stacks of money every night at closing. My parents put in long hours to keep the business running. They worked very hard and it was common for my mom, or my dad—or both—to come home around 2:00 or 2:30a.m. after closing the restaurant. But one night my dad stayed later than usual at the restaurant.

My mother was home with my brother that night. She told him that she was going to stop by the restaurant.

Years later, when I was 13, I found out the truth about that night. My mother had a deep suspicion—an uneasy feeling in her stomach that wouldn't go away.

That feeling prompted her to visit the restaurant late at night. When she arrived, she went upstairs to a small room with a bed where the staff would rest during their breaks. She walked to the door, opened it without knocking—and found my father in the act of adultery with the other couple's wife. Of all people, he chose to betray her with the adulterous wife of their business partner. What an outrageous, selfish, and destructive act!

My mother was crushed in every way, watching the man she loved, married, and had two children with commit adultery right in front of her eyes. What a disgraceful and damaging image. Even now, talking about it stirs up painful emotions.

After I found out at the age of 13, I had to learn to forgive quickly just to survive under the same roof with him, my mother, and my brother. Because of my father's affair with the co-owner's wife, my mother decided to sell our half of the restaurant back to them and move us back to Maryland.

A thought for people who are thinking about committing adultery. Do not do it!!!

Not only are you going to destroy your partner emotionally, psychologically, spiritually, and physically—your children are also going to be deeply affected. They will develop feelings of rejection, low self-esteem, bitterness, hatred, unforgiveness, and anger.

You will completely alter the psychological makeup of your children. It will affect their growth and hinder their ability to communicate with others, as well as their overall outlook on life.

It will impact their lifestyle and decisions. Often, they are led down paths involving drugs and other harmful addictions.

Because of the pain depression causes, if children do not receive proper, Godly counseling from an experienced pastor, they may turn to destructive and temporary solutions. In other words, your children can easily end up in gangs, criminal activity, drug abuse, theft, and other dangerous behaviors.

Really ask yourself: Is a night of sin and adultery worth ruining your family and your life?

If you struggle with uncontrollable lust, you need to seek a pastor who is experienced in deliverance. Liberation comes when a person filled with the Holy Spirit lays hands on you and casts the spirit of lust out of your body.

An evil spirit cannot be removed through psychological or psychiatric counseling alone. Spirits only obey and submit to the name of Jesus. I was not freed from the spirit of depression until a pastor and two ministers prayed over me and cast that demon out. As they prayed, I fell backward and saw two dark shadows leave my body.

When those demons of depression and alcohol were cast out, I felt an enormous weight lift from me. I was completely healed and delivered. I stopped drinking that day. I was no longer depressed.

My entire outlook on life changed in an instant. God is real— and He loves us. He desires to set everyone free.

CHAPTER 3

Moving Back Home to Maryland

I was thrilled to move back to Maryland. Philadelphia could have been a victorious financial blessing, but it was ruined by one man's greed, lust, selfishness, and adultery. I never felt comfortable there—especially since all my friends were back in Maryland. I also knew I would be free from the physical abuse of the nuns in Catholic school. With that in mind, I was eager and ready to move back to Maryland.

Back to school

I was the only Hispanic kid in my entire neighborhood, which led to a lot of bullying and racism in my life. I already had enough drama at home to last ten lifetimes; I certainly didn't need bullies at school picking on me for being of Spanish origin. I had to repeat the third grade.

This time, the bullying at school was different. Instead of nuns hitting me, I now had to deal with fifth graders who were bigger than me.

There always seems to be one bad apple in the bunch. There was a huge bully who was much taller than all of us—another Goliath that I had to confront.

I already had two Goliaths at home to contend with. I did not need the added burden of bullying and racism in my life.

Every day at lunch, this bully—who looked like he was 7 feet tall—asked me for my lunch money. He would say, "Give me your lunch money or else." Everybody knew what "or else" meant. I had to give up my one dollar for lunch every day. At one point, after I'd had enough of the abuse, I told my mom. I'm still not sure if that was a clever idea but I felt like I had no choice at the time.

My mom was called to the principal's office for a meeting with me, the boy, and his mother. The principal only gave him one week of detention and said, "Do not do that again." He wasn't threatened with expulsion or any serious punishment.

I was left alone—without anyone demanding my lunch money—for about a month. But after a few short weeks, I had to deal with three or four other bullies, who thought it was funny to call me racial slurs.

This really hurt my feelings. I felt even more rejection, pain, and affliction than I had ever experienced. I did not want to go to school anymore. The fear I lived with during that time was overwhelming. I already had a strong fear of my older brother. I also had a nervous fear of my mother's backhanded slaps to my face. And now, on top of that, I feared the bullies whose prejudice added to my pain.

I asked my mother if I could be homeschooled, but she couldn't afford it. Her answer was a clear no. She told me to fight back. But how could I fight a six-foot giant when I was only four-something and skinny? I didn't even consider hitting back—I was afraid I could get my bones broken, or something worse.

The bullies would follow me home on their bicycles after school. Three or four of them would wait until I stopped near someone's front yard, then they would push me off my bike. Once I was on the ground, they would start kicking me, punching me, and calling me "spic." This bullying went on until early ninth grade.

In the ninth grade, I met a good friend who had a lot of courage and was also bullied. When I spent time with my new friend, the bullying became less severe. The bullies in those days used to also chew tobacco. They would fill their hands with tobacco saliva, and throw it on the back of my shirt and in my hair.

This went on for several weeks. I told my friend I couldn't take it anymore and wanted to drop out of school. My friend said, "Do not worry, I have an idea to solve this situation." A few days later, I noticed that the bullying had completely stopped. I was thrilled and so happy. I never asked my friend what he did to make it stop; I was simply grateful that it was over.

After high school graduation, my friend moved far away, and we lost contact after some years. It's as if God put him there just so I could finish my high school education.

I do not think I could have finished high school because of all the bullying I endured, if it hadn't been for him.

The boat ride from hell

My mom and dad had a friend who owned a boat on the Chesapeake Bay. It was a nice boat, about 26 feet in length, with a steering wheel on the main cabin floor, and another on the fly deck. From time to time, he would invite me and my family on a boat ride. One summer day, he invited my mother, my brother, and I to go out on the bay.

I was 15 years old when I went on this boat ride. I remember it was a nice sunny day, about 75 degrees. My brother and I were steering the boat from the fly deck. Meanwhile, my mother and this friend of hers were drinking liquor on the main deck. Nothing seemed to be out of the ordinary—or so I thought.

It gets hot out on the water in a boat, with the sun beaming down during the summertime. My brother asked if I could go downstairs and get us something to drink. I said, "Sure, I'll be right back." I lowered myself down the ladder that led to the main deck, and I was shocked to find my mom's breast completely out with the man's lips on it. When my mother noticed me, she quickly pulled her breast in and covered her front with the blouse she had on.

But it was too late to cover it up. I had just seen the most horrific image that any teenager can imagine.

My heart was broken and my emotions were all over the place. I really wanted to punch that guy in the face—so badly. I went up the ladder with my heart racing extremely fast.

I told my brother what I saw. He was silent for a good 30 seconds; I could see his face contort with anger. When he got mad, he would bite the inside of his cheek. I asked my brother what he was going to do about it. I thought he was going to confront the man and knock him out—at least, right? That's not what happened. My brother replied, "I will talk with Mom later."

I couldn't believe the passive reaction my brother had to such a traumatizing, vile event. There was no excuse for not confronting either of them at that moment.

When we got home from the hellish ride on the boat, my brother told me later that night that he confronted our mother about her sick behavior. She denied the whole thing and claimed nothing ever happened. This was typical of her—to deny any wrongdoing.

When my brother told me this, I felt sick to my stomach. I felt like I never wanted to see my mother again. I grew bitter towards her and did not forgive her for many years after this happened.

I did not have the willpower to forgive my mother until I accepted Jesus as my Savior at the age of 25. That was ten years after the incident happened.

This experience became one of many factors that led me to leave home at the age of 17.

My brothers abuse gets worse

My mom and dad used to go away on weekends—either to a friend's log cabin or to play poker. While they were away, my brother was usually in charge of watching me. Occasionally, my mom would splurge on a babysitter if he was out with his friends on some weekends.

I remember one night when he invited a friend downstairs to his room while my parents were away, and he was supposed to be watching me. He told me not to come to his room and to stay upstairs and watch TV.

When we're young, we can get curious at the worst times. I stayed upstairs for a little while but eventually got up and walked toward the basement door, opening it slowly. I started to walk down the steps carefully, trying not to make any noise. I decided to spy on them—that was an unbelievably bad decision.

I smelled a strange odor coming from my brother's room. later in life, I found out that the odor was marijuana.

My brother burst out of his bedroom, grabbed me under my arm, picked me up, and took me to my bedroom upstairs. He tied me up with my hands behind my back, tied my feet together, and hung me upside down by the doorknob. Afterwards, he shoved a sock in my mouth and tied it behind my head.

This is called kidnapping ladies and gentlemen!

He left me hanging upside down by the doorknob with my hands and feet tied.

Apart from the obvious trauma, I wonder what hanging a 10-year-old upside down by a doorknob for half an hour would do to his brain. I am extremely fortunate to still be alive and in good mental health. I give all the glory to Jesus Christ, who healed all my wounds and trauma.

Kidnapping is a felony in the state of Maryland, punishable by up to 30 years in jail.

My brother left me hanging upside down by the doorknob for at least half an hour. He did this to me several times. It always seemed to happen when he had that friend over. I guess he didn't want me telling our parents that I smelled a strange odor coming from his room. Even though I wouldn't have told on him anyway, the fear he instilled in me was enough to keep me silent.

He would always tie me up and gag me so I couldn't scream, then lock me in the closet for up to an hour or more. To this day, I cannot be in tight spaces—I start to hyperventilate and have panic attacks if I'm too confined.

My brother always told me after these horrendous acts that if I ever told our mother or father, it would be worse next time. I never told them.

Chapter 3

The purpose of sharing this now—about being kidnapped—is to show the reader that no matter what kind of hell you've gone through, Jesus can and does heal all wounds. For healing to happen, we must earnestly seek Him and invite Him to live in our hearts.

The creepy idol

My mother had an idol that an old man gave her when she was a 9 year old child. This idol stood about 5 inches tall and had its own little enclosure to stand in. The name of this idol was St. John Bosque. The old man told my mother that it was the saint that watched over young children.

Every time there was a crisis or something to be prayed for, my mother would light a candle in front of this idol. When she lit the candle, the atmosphere in the house would instantly change and you could feel the evil spirits brushing up against you. It was very scary, and I could sense the evil that emanated from the idol.

On several occasions, my mother would light the candle in front of this so-called saint. Then her eyes would turn from caramel brown—her normal eye color—to pitch black, with almost no white around the pupils. This terrified me the first time, and every other time I saw it happen.

My mother would turn to me, and in a man's, voice would say, "What's wrong with you?" She had a very angry demeanor when this happened. I would start to stutter and say, "Nothing mom, I just want to go out for little while." I would leave the house and not come back till hours later. I never told anybody about this while it was happening because I did not want the bullies at school to start giving me a tough time and laughing at the situation. I learned my lesson to not tell anybody anything about my personal life during these troubled times.

This turning of the eye color to black and the voice of a woman turning into a man's voice, whenever a candle was lit in front of the idol, happened on several occasions.

One day, I grabbed that idol and broke it around the neck. I knew beyond any doubt that it was evil, and I wanted to destroy it. When my mother got home and saw the idol with its neck cracked and pieces missing, she went into a fit of anger. I told her I had accidentally dropped it while dusting, to avoid punishment. I was fortunate not to get smacked for it, and she told me never to touch her demonic idol again. I apologized to my mother and told her I would never touch it again.

Knowing what I know now, the right thing to do would have been to smash it into pieces and throw it in the trash. But I would have been kicked out of the house if I had done that. However, many years later, I did get the opportunity—along with a few members of the church—to go into a witch's house after she had accepted Jesus as Savior and smash idols that looked like the one my mom had. I then learned that these idols were considered evil because witches use them to make satanic altars. They use idols in the image of Jesus, the Virgin Mary, and others. These were some of the idols I got to smash and throw into a trash bag after the now ex-witch accepted Jesus.

I know from years of studying the Bible, reading books by former warlocks who are now Christian evangelists, and from my own experiences, that there are one or more demons behind every idol or graven image.

Why would any educated, rational person want demons in their house? This kind of ignorance is dangerous and invites curses instead of blessings into a person's life.

CHAPTER 4

Leaving The Psycho House at 17

In the mid-80s, a teenager at the age of 17 and a half could legally leave their parents' house if they had written permission from their parents stating it was okay. I finally had a chance to do what I had dreamt about for years: to get out of that house. I was finally going to escape from the house of horror—I could almost taste the freedom.

Out on my own for the first time.

I began life on my own at 17 years of age. I had no college degree, technical training, or experience in any trade.

I was afflicted with small fiber neuropathy, depression, and trauma from all I had endured in the house of horror. I looked in the local paper and finally found a room. The freedom I needed and deserved was now closer than ever.

I rented a room in College Park, Maryland, near the University of Maryland. The house was rented to three students who were attending the university a mile away.

I got a job nearby at Bally's health club selling memberships. There, I met a group of friends with some unhealthy habits that were similar to mine.

On weekends, we would go out to the closest bar, have a few drinks, and find out how we could get drugs. Alcohol and marijuana were my drugs of choice. I used these substances to numb the neuropathic pain that afflicted me.

After the experience of the boat from hell and my mother's adultery, I started drinking heavily and smoking pot as well. A harder drug entered the picture, but when I used it, it made me extremely nervous because it caused my heart to beat incredibly fast. I stayed away from it as much as possible, although I still used it from time to time.

Depression is painful—it drains energy, focus, and the desire to carry out the most necessary tasks of everyday life. Studies estimate that as many as half of all people with depression in the U.S. go undiagnosed or untreated. In the case of my small fiber neuropathy, I eventually had to take strong painkillers to manage the pain in later years.

When a person is depressed, they are in a very vulnerable state of mind and will try just about anything that promises to quickly alleviate the physical and psychological pain they're experiencing.

To be free from any ailment, a person must first ask for forgiveness of all sins and then invite the healer—Jesus—into their heart. I did not have this opportunity until I was 25. I first went to see a doctor, which is better than taking no action at all.

The next step in the healing process is to find a pastor who is filled with the Holy Spirit and has experience casting out evil spirits. Tell him what ails you. If you do not know, find a good physician and get an analysis. Then go to the pastor and tell him the name of the disease so that he knows what to pray against.

The afflicted person needs the evil spirits that have them bound to be cast out in Jesus' name. I was not completely delivered until the evil spirits of depression and drug addiction were cast out of me. The final step is to see a good doctor and receive the physical medicine they prescribe to help balance any chemical deficiencies.

Jesus can also take care of the medical aspect. However, He may leave the chemical and medical part of the healing to a doctor. God uses doctors to address the scientific and medical aspects of disease.

Luke 4:23 reads, "Those who are well do not need a physician, but those who are sick."

2 Kings 20:7 says, "Isaiah said, 'take a lump of figs,' and they took and laid it on the boil, and he recovered."

The Bible clearly approves of and uses physicians. The next verse supports the authority that God has given to His followers. This includes all who have received Jesus as Savior and follow His word.

Matthew 10:1 says, "Jesus called His twelve disciples to Him and gave them authority to drive out impure spirits and to heal every disease and sickness."

"Every disease and sickness" means there is no illness that God cannot heal. A disciple is simply someone who follows and practices the teachings of Jesus.

The difficulties of keeping a job and functioning in society

With the combination of small fiber neuropathy, depression, and trauma afflicting me, it was exceedingly difficult to keep a job.

One of the effects of abuse is an unhealthy disrespect for or indifference to authority. For example, if I had a boss who raised his voice or mistreated me in any way, the trauma would be triggered and amplified, and I would immediately want to leave the job. I had no tolerance for yelling or any other abusive behavior. I simply wasn't going to accept it.

We all know that in life we must put up with difficult people in the workplace. If you work in customer service—as I did—you encounter difficult people all day long. But the trauma, small fiber neuropathy, and depression I was dealing with made it impossible for me to hold any kind of job.

I did not seek counseling until the age of 13, when I found out that my mother wanted to divorce my dad because of the adultery he committed in Philadelphia. I sometimes strongly suspect that Philadelphia was not the only time my dad was unfaithful to my mom.

Counseling helped me by giving me someone to talk to—it gave me an outlet to get things off my chest. I was also prescribed medication to help balance the chemical deficiencies that contributed to my depression. At that time, effective medications for depression were not yet widely available. The medicine I was prescribed helped a little. Thirteen years later, as medical treatments improved, I was switched to something that worked much better.

As for neuropathy, I was self-medicating with alcohol and pot to dull the pain. I believed the pain I felt was normal because my mother had said that we all go through pain; therefore, I believed the pins and needles from the neuropathy were normal. I did not seek help for neuropathy until several years later, when the pain became unbearable and more severe.

At this point, I could no longer self-medicate because the pain had increased to an intolerable, more intense level. This is when I went to speak to a pain specialist for help.

The doctor diagnosed me with small fiber neuropathy. I had never heard of this disease. First, he tried all the non-narcotic pain medications, but none of them were effective—they did not take the pain away.

I had no choice but to go on narcotic painkillers. I strongly tried to avoid these because I had heard many negative stories about how people become dependent on them and how they can harm the liver.

Even with the help of counseling and pain management doctors, I was not delivered from the evil spirits behind these illnesses. I still had symptoms of depression and continued to feel the pain of pins and needles between doses. Only part of the problem was resolved. I did function better with the pain medication and the new medicine for depression. The problem with these two medications was that they caused drowsiness. So, they helped on one hand but drained my energy on the other.

Being out in the world and trying to hold down a job to pay for room, board, and food with these kinds of ailments was next to impossible. Living alone and trying to support myself day to day was a challenging task. As far as the medical world was concerned, I was as healed as I was going to get.

Thank God that Jesus Christ stepped into my life at the age of 25. If it were not for the casting out of those demons—depression and alcoholism—I would only be, at best, 40% better. The other

60% that prayer accomplished was necessary for me to be completely restored and healthy.

Only by going to an experienced minister who practices casting out evil spirits through prayer and the power of the Holy Spirit can someone be totally healed and delivered. I know this is a fact because it happened to me.

If a person who has depression—or any other ailment—only takes medicine prescribed by a physician, they will never be fully delivered or completely healed.

There is a physical realm, and there is also a spiritual realm, which few people understand. A person must embrace both if they want to be whole and live in health.

One example I can give is this: A person can have a nicely waxed car with beautiful paint on the outside, but if the engine and transmission are not in good working condition, the car will only look good temporarily and soon break down. In the same way, if the spiritual aspect of illness is not addressed, the person will not be complete or fully healthy.

Thank God for medication, but it is only part of the solution. God placed doctors here to help humanity, and He uses them for His glory—to help us. Doctors are friends of God. I do not believe that a person who takes medication is any less of a Christian or has less faith than another believer who does not take medicine. That is a false concept. God clearly uses doctors to heal the sick.

If that pastor and those ministers had not prayed for me and rebuked the spirits of alcohol and depression, I would not be as fully healed as I am today. I have lived this truth and know without a doubt that evil spirits must be expelled for a person to be liberated and completely healed.

CHAPTER 5

The Encounter with Jesus That Blessed My Life Forever

The year was 1995. I rented a room in a house from an elderly Jewish woman. She was a genuinely nice lady who invited me to go to church one Sunday. I embarrassingly declined and said, "One day I will go." I could have told her, "No, I am not interested please do not ask me again," but God was tugging at my heart. As a child, I was taught to respect church, elderly people, and God.

Growing up as a Catholic, we were taught to respect our elders and learn from them. I was living a life that was going to lead me to jail, the hospital, or the graveyard.

I could discern that if I did not change my ways soon, I was surely going to die and be in danger of eternal hell.

All my acquaintances were drug addicts who were barely holding on to sanity and had no goals in life. They lived life from one day to another and one addiction to another.

I will talk about how important it is to change who you acquaint yourself with in a later chapter.

At this point in my life, I knew I had to choose between God's path or the road to perdition. Do I continue this self-destructive road of addiction, anger, and rebellion, or do I lace up my combat boots and find a solution to this insane, unproductive lifestyle?

The lady from whom I rented a room continued to invite me to church, and I continued to put it off. When we are in a negative or traumatic situation, part of us procrastinates and avoids confronting our issues. But our better sense tells us we must face them—or pay a heavy price.

Weeks passed. It was summertime in August. The landlady asked me again if I wanted to go to church. This time, without even thinking, I said, "Yes, okay. I will go." I had no intention of saying yes—it just poured out of me. She had asked me on a Saturday afternoon and said, "Great, the service starts at 11 tomorrow. We can go then, if that's okay?"

I replied, "Yes, that will be fine."

There was a Pentecostal church that was temporarily renting the auditorium at Richard Montgomery High School because their church was being renovated.

The church was separated, meaning that women were on the left side and the men were on the right side. I was the only man in the service, and there were approximately seven elderly ladies on the women's side. I sat down on the right side by myself and listened to the pastor's sermon, which had started at 11 a.m.

I felt a unique presence in this church that I had not experienced in any other. It was a combination of strong energy and love. This was my first time visiting a Pentecostal church.

At the end of the sermon, the pastor invited people who wanted prayer to go to the front. In the prayer line, I saw most of the women get up and go to meet the pastor.

I was contemplating whether I should humble myself and go to the prayer line or stay in my seat. Suddenly, my knees started to shake and vibrate. I felt a power that I had never felt before, pulling me to get up and go to the front. The power was so strong that I could hardly resist it. I was sitting down when I suddenly felt someone touch my right shoulder. In an instant, I was standing upright, without exerting any energy of my own. Remember, I was the only man sitting there, and no one was behind me. It was an angel that miraculously stood me to my feet.

I knew this was the power of the real God and that He was calling me to be born again.

I was nervous as I walked forward to the prayer line. Only three women remained in front of me. I don't know if I was more excited or nervous—I was both. Finally, it was my turn to pray with the pastor. He asked me if I would like to receive Jesus as my Lord and Savior. I responded yes.

A simple prayer to accept Jesus as Lord and Savior, inviting him into your heart.

The pastor had me repeat the following prayer:

Dear Jesus, _I believe that you died and rose again to pay for my sins. You are seated in heaven at the right hand of the Father. I ask you to wash me clean and forgive me for all my sins. Jesus, I open my heart and invite you in, to be my Lord and Savior. Amen._

When I said, "I open my heart and invite you in," the whole ceiling of the auditorium disappeared, and I saw a clear blue sky. Jesus appeared, smiling with His arms open. He was dressed in a glowing white robe. I had never experienced anything like this. I fell to the floor backward, feeling light as a feather. The ministers caught me. I was not hurt when I fell. I later found out that this is called being "slain in the Spirit."

I was on the floor for 5 to 10 minutes. Then I started to open my eyes as the ministers helped me to my feet. I felt a tremendous peace and was exceptionally light, as if I could almost fly away. The pastor asked me if I would like more prayer and said we could go to the back room. I replied yes, with a big smile on my face. I thought to myself, If this is prayer, I want more. Most of the women had left the auditorium by then. The pastor, two ministers, and I went backstage, behind the pulpit and curtains.

The ministers and the pastor joined in prayer. They laid hands on me and yelled, "Spirit of depression and alcohol, I bind you in Jesus' name. Get out!"

At that moment, I had my eyes wide open, and I saw two dark shadow figures—about 1½ feet tall—leave my body and disappear. The demons had finally been completely expelled from my body, in the name of Jesus.

I felt even lighter than before, as if a huge weight had been lifted off my heart. I instantly sensed in my spirit that complete liberation from the demons of depression and alcoholism had just occurred. I had never felt better in all my life. I had finally received the spiritual freedom I needed.

The truth is that Jesus is the solution to depression and any other spirits of sickness that are traumatizing and binding your life. I am a living testimony that people can be healed from any evil spirit that is keeping them sick and bound. The sickness can be either physical or mental—it makes absolutely no difference—because God heals the mind, body, soul, and spirit.

This is one of my physical healings.

I tore a tendon in my elbow while lifting weights. It was swollen for about two weeks and very painful. I couldn't even slightly use a hammer or do anything that might cause any impact to my right arm. I humbled myself in prayer and asked God to please heal my elbow.

Suddenly, when I put my left hand on my right elbow, my arm started vibrating, and at once, the pain disappeared, along with the swelling.

Afterward, I went to a client's house to see how well my arm worked. I shoveled their entire driveway, which had two feet of snow. It took me almost two hours to shovel because of the size of the driveway.

The client knew I had hurt my elbow and could not believe I was shoveling snow. I was already witnessing to the client, proving that healing still happens today—and every day.

Fellowshipping and how it increased my faith.

I had a friend who invited me to fellowship at his church. Gladly, I accepted the invitation, greatly desiring to know more about the God I had just accepted as my Savior and Healer.

Attending church and Bible study really helped me get rooted in His Word as a young believer. Looking back on my life, I now realize that group prayer, studying the Bible, and congregating were what kept me grounded and strengthened my faith during those trying, turbulent years. I had been delivered from the spirits that were binding me and knew I had to keep the fire of God burning and growing inside me daily.

This was a detrimental and essential part of my healing recovery. Had I not congregated, I would have been in danger of becoming lukewarm and falling back into old addictions and unhealthy relationships. The devil cannot manipulate a Christian who is on fire for God and who keeps the flame of salvation and the Holy Spirit burning strong in their heart.

If you have a log in a fire, and that log is no longer red-hot, it becomes easier to grab and manipulate. This symbolizes how we are as Christians: if we grow lukewarm or cold in our spirit by neglecting to congregate, pray, and study the Bible, it will surely lead to backsliding and returning to the bondage from which God delivered us.

I have seen new believers begin to associate with unsaved, worldly friends after accepting Jesus. Sadly, many fell right back into drugs, partying, and committing crimes.

We must remain on fire and filled with God's Holy Spirit if we want to experience lasting deliverance and live a holy, prosperous, and positive life.

I cannot emphasize enough how important it is to congregate with a group of believers. Staying connected with mature Christians is essential. But do not seek perfection in anyone—perfection is a fleeting illusion. Remember, as soon as Peter took his eyes off Jesus, he began to sink. If we overly esteem people and focus on them instead of Jesus, we too will sink. The only perfect person is Jesus. Keeping our focus on Him is how we grow spiritually and gain stability in every area of life.

The Bible clearly tells us that no one is perfect or righteous except Jesus. Romans 3:23 says, "All have sinned and come short of the glory of God." To reach God's perfect will for our lives, we must still strive to be holy—meaning, set apart from the world and the traps it disguises as fun.

You can find mature Christians in the church or even at your workplace. What matters most is staying close to people who are on fire for God. The Spirit of God is not only holy—it is a power-house of positive energy, and we desperately need it to succeed in life.

Try not to surround yourself with negative people, as their influence will quench the positive outlook God has given you through His Holy Spirit. I know this to be true because I experienced it during my early years as a new Christian.

Listening to and being around negative people will absolutely drain your spirit. They are like vacuums that lead you into a bottomless pit—constantly sapping your spiritual energy until you feel exhausted and discouraged. Their poisonous conversations can leave you feeling hopeless and depressed.

Finding new Godly friends after receiving Jesus

Another especially important thing I did after receiving Jesus was finding Christian friends. It wasn't as hard as I had imagined. God removed people from my life who were not good for my spiritual growth. In some cases, He moved them to another state, or they would suddenly stop calling.

It amazed me how superficial my acquaintances really were after I stopped drinking and using drugs. Ungodly people stay around when things are good and your pockets are full of money.

When things go bad and you need someone to talk to, worldly acquaintances quickly disappear and are nowhere to be found.

I can guarantee that the minute you stop hanging out at clubs and going out drinking, the group of acquaintances you thought were your friends will quickly distance themselves from you. One test I did was inviting my so-called friends to church. If they wanted nothing to do with church, I just stopped calling them. Amazingly—and sure enough—they stopped calling me too.

From this point on the Lord separated me effortlessly from bad influences which were really acquaintances and not friends. He started putting a couple of quality people in my life, one being a pastor which has been a beacon to me in my spiritual growth.

It is always an advantage when you find somebody spiritually mature that can see way beyond what you see in the spirit realm. They can teach you how to fight your spiritual battles by praying and fasting. God did not put a large crowd of people in my life as friends. Experience and time revealed to me that it is not the quantity of people around you but the quality.

I had lost all my acquaintances, and at first, I thought I would be sad. In the beginning, I was. But as weeks turned into months, I realized I was better off with no friends than with fake ones. Keeping my focus on Jesus was another key to breaking away from ungodly relationships.

The more time you spend seeking God, the more you will realize He is more satisfying to talk to than anyone else.

You'll find that His love is immeasurable and that He cares about every aspect of your life. He wants to be your best friend—far more than you can imagine.

I realized how much time I had wasted in the world, forming ungodly relationships with unhealthy people.

Spending time with God helps keep us focused on staying on the straight and narrow path. Communicating with God in prayer as much as possible is key to discovering our destiny. He loves us so deeply that He fills every void in our hearts with His perfect love and peace.

People immersed in sin do not want to be around someone who is constantly growing in fellowship with Jesus. As **James 4:7** says, "Resist the devil, and he will flee from you."

The healing process is a journey of making quality decisions.

Being healed from childhood trauma is a process. It requires constant forward movement, proactive choices, and seeking God, which produces spiritual growth and health. The Bible tells us that faith comes by hearing the Word. The more we hear God's Word, the more the tree of faith inside us grows, making us stronger and healthier. **Psalm 107:20** says, "He sent His word and healed them." God's Word has the power to heal us.

This healing process includes congregating at church, studying God's Word, fellowshipping, praying, and fasting. Talking to God as a friend—as opposed to only asking Him for things—is both productive and necessary for our spiritual and physical well-being and maturity.

Praying and fasting cultivate a personal relationship that God wants to have with each of us. For example, just as we grow our marriage by spending time with our spouse, we grow closer to God by spending time with Him. As a result, we begin to know Him more deeply. Our relationship with Him, like a marriage, will be fortified by the quality time we invest in it.

The closer we grow to God, the easier the walk becomes. The demons may still attack, but their attacks grow weaker and less effective. Living in a close relationship with our heavenly Father produces anointing and spiritual strength.

The more time you spend with someone, the better you get to know them—and deeper, stronger, quality friendships will blossom.

Growing in the knowledge of anything takes time. When the seed of God's Word is planted in our hearts, it begins a process.

It won't be long before spiritual transformation starts to occur.

The more time we spend in God's Word, the faster our spiritual growth and healing will take place. I remained faithful in attending church and studying the Bible throughout my healing process. I know that if I had not stayed committed to these vital steps, I would not have received healing or gained victory over trauma. I also may never have been called to ministry later in life.

The key to health is giving God all of our heart—because He gave everything for us when He died on the cross at Calvary. God knows whether we are sincere. He hears every thought we have before it even enters our mind.

We cannot expect everything from God—healing, blessings, and the fulfillment of His promises—if we are not willing to give all of ourselves fully to Him. We must be sincere in our decision to trust Him and follow the path He has already laid out for us.

God heals a person's leg at a Bible study

I was invited to a Bible study one Wednesday night, and I gladly accepted the invitation. At the end of the Bible study, a sister who had a sore knee asked me if I could please pray for it.

I asked her if I could place my hand on her knee. She replied, "Yes." When I laid my right hand on her and prayed, she was healed instantly. She was in tears because there was no longer tormenting pain in her once-damaged knee. I felt a heart full of joy after God healed this woman's knee. This moment sparked my growing interest in the gifts of healing and miracles.

Matthew 10:7,8 says, "And as you go, preach, saying, 'The kingdom of heaven is at hand.' Heal the sick, raise the dead, cleanse the lepers, cast out demons. Freely you have received; freely give."

CHAPTER 6

My Calling to The Ministry At Age 33

I had been fellowshipping in a Pentecostal church in Washington, DC, for a little more than half a decade. I would attend services 3 to 4 days per week during this six-year period. During this time, I was growing spiritually and receiving valuable education. The day I never imagined I would see had finally come.

During the summertime of 1998, an evangelist by the name of Dr. Hector de la Cruz was invited by my pastor to preach at our church.

God used this man tremendously in the miracle ministry. He held a doctorate in divinity and was very humble, wise, and most importantly, filled with and guided by the Holy Spirit.

He had been in the ministry for 15 years and this gave him a wealth of experience. The Lord often used brother Hector in the gift of prophecy. He would call out someone's name in the congregation—people he had never met—and begin telling them details about their lives. It was amazing to see how God worked through him.

It was about 7 PM when the church service started. That night, four or five churches from different areas had gathered together. Many people in the Christian community already knew how God used Brother Hector in healing, miracles, and teaching the Word of God.

The church service began with praise and worship. Afterwards, Dr. Hector De la Cruz came to the pulpit and began his sermon.

He gave the church two verses from the Bible and began to preach. Fifteen minutes into the sermon, he paused and pointed in my direction. He said, "The young man," and a brother to my right replied, "Me?" Hector responded, "No, the tall guy standing next to you." It was me he was pointing at. This was a surreal moment for me.

He continued, saying, "Thus says the Lord: I am giving you a ministry and opening a door that no man can shut. You will fulfill the plans I have for you. I have given you the key to this city." I was amazed and speechless.

He called me to come up to the pulpit. He was drinking an orange sports drink from a glass. Pouring more into the glass, he handed it to me and said, "Let us celebrate your ministry." I took a drink and handed it back to him. He drank from it, then raised it up, giving thanks to God. I was standing five feet away, and without him touching me, I fell out in the Spirit when he raised the glass. The power of God came over me, and I gently fell to the floor. After a minute or so, the brothers picked me up. I felt light as a feather and filled with joy.

I was overwhelmed after the short ceremony of blessing the ministry that God had just given me. It was like something out of a movie. I did not expect this to happen.

If we are faithful, God truly desires to give us everything our hearts desire, according to His will.

God did not forget the wishes I had as a young boy—dreams of hearing His voice and becoming a leader in the church. As I matured, I came to understand that He truly does care about our ambitions and dreams. Jesus is more than ready to fulfill them if we are sincere and willing.

The years I spent at this church had produced the right fruit. Being called out by a well-known prophet pointed me in a new direction.

A thought from the past

I was 11 years old when I attended Catholic church with my mom and dad. I remember asking my mom, "How does the priest know so much about God?" She replied, "He hears God's voice." I thought to myself, Wow, what a privilege it would be to hear God. Since that moment, I wanted to be a leader in the church.

My mother said, "Remember, you cannot get married if you are a priest." It made me sad to hear this. I didn't know that pastors and ministers could get married—or even what a pastor or minister was. My mother never mentioned another religion where the preacher could get married or that it was even possible. Ignorance can ruin a person's destiny; it almost destroyed mine.

My first missionary trip, to the Dominican Republic.

I was invited to go to the Dominican Republic on a missionary trip by a friend from church. I gladly accepted the invitation. Going on a missionary trip was something I had wanted to do since childhood.

When we arrived, I visited a Pentecostal church. After the sermon, I was introduced to a lady pastor.

Once the service ended, she prophesied that God wanted me to visit her and her husband at their home. I prayed about it, and I received confirmation from the Lord to go. This pastor was one of the nicest people I had ever met—very genuine and humble. I was curious to meet her husband and fellowship with them.

I told Paul, the person I went to the church with, where I was going, and he freaked out. He said the neighborhood where the pastor lived was so dangerous that even the police wouldn't go there. He explained that gangs in the area carried machetes, which they sharpened on both sides—mocking the Bible verse that says God's word is sharper than a two-edged sword.

I said, "I respect your knowledge and warning, but I must go because God sent me there. I must do what He tells me." Paul had been with me for the entire missionary trip, but he was afraid to go to that neighborhood and visit the pastor and her husband. Then his cousins also tried to persuade us not to go.

There were five days left before we were to visit the pastor. It was a tense time because many people did not want Paul or me to go. The neighborhood was six hours away by bus. Finally, the day of departure arrived. The trip was uncomfortable—the bus was old and worn out, and the drivers liked to speed, which I really didn't like.

We arrived at three in the afternoon. As Paul and I got off the bus, we saw seven or eight gang members standing around with machetes in their hands. I said to Paul, "Let us pray." He humbly bowed his head, and we began to pray, asking for God's protection and help. When we opened our eyes, the men looked as if they had seen a ghost. They panicked and ran in all directions away from where we were going. It was as if they vanished—we never saw them again during the entire trip. I imagine they saw our guardian angels with swords drawn. The bible says, "No weapon formed against us shall prosper." God never forsakes His sons or His word.

Paul and I arrived at Pastor Griselda's house after a short 10-minute walk. As we approached the back door, Pastor Griselda came out to greet us with a big smile and gave us both a hug. Her husband followed behind and also greeted us warmly. They invited us to sit down and asked if we would like something to drink. I asked for a glass of water, and Paul had one as well.

We conversed for a while, and I found out that they had been fasting for five days—not by choice, but because they did not have any food. When I heard this, we immediately went to the store and bought as much food as we could, filling the refrigerator. You can imagine how happy they were after not eating for five days.

Henry, Griselda's husband, had just lost his job, and times were exceedingly difficult. Griselda was pastoring full-time at a church composed mostly of junior high and high school students. The children didn't work, as they were in school full-time.

Pastor Griselda depended on Henry's job and the small offerings the children would give at church when they could. What little they had went toward paying the rent for the church building.

We stayed with the pastor and her husband for a couple of days. We had an amazing time fellowshipping with them. They were two of the nicest people I had ever met. When it was time to return to the city, Santo Domingo, we shared a final lunch and prayed together for a safe trip back.

Back in the city

We congregated with Pastor Ramon at a church called El Casique. After a weekday church service, Paul and I were invited to go on a leaders' retreat near the border of Haiti and the Dominican Republic. We eagerly accepted the invitation. God always kept me busy congregating and visiting churches while I was on this missionary trip with Brother Paul.

The day came when we left Santo Domingo on a ten-hour bus ride, heading toward the border of Haiti.

It was a beautiful tropical day, as it usually is in this part of the world. The only thing I did not like about the bus ride was that it was a public bus, and the driver was drinking a beer while driving at 80 mph. This made me extremely nervous. I was not used to this kind of speed—especially with the driver drinking. It was completely unacceptable.

After about 10 minutes of this reckless driving, I had had enough. I got out of my seat and told the driver to slow down or I would report him to the authorities. He replied, "You do not have to do that. I will slow down."

Talk about putting your life in danger—with an intoxicated bus driver going 80 miles per hour, passing cars on a two-lane, two-directional road.

The fact that I was in another country was not going to deter me from speaking up for my rights.

Where I saw my first miracle.

We finally arrived at the place where we were going to stay. It was in a heavily wooded area near the border of the Dominican Republic and Haiti. The place was very peaceful—I felt as though

I had gone back in time a thousand years. The people living there were very humble, friendly, and polite.

After securing our belongings in our sleeping quarters, we gathered and prayed. The other ministers and I decided to do a two-day fast. We arrived on a Friday afternoon and left Sunday afternoon. On the second day, a group of five of us decided to go for a walk. After about fifteen minutes, we stopped to drink some water.

A very elderly woman—I'd say in her 90s—approached us, walking with a 90-degree bend in her back that began at her waist. She asked if we could please pray for her. Her back was so hunched that she could barely make eye contact. We all looked at each other and said, "Yes, we will pray for you."

We had a habit of closing our eyes while praying. With all our eyes closed, we prayed. When we opened them, to our complete amazement, she was standing completely upright—no bend in her back at all. Tears flowed down her face as she thanked us for the prayer. I spoke up and said, "It was not us—it was Jesus who healed you. Let us thank Him for the miracle together."

The woman smiled and walked away so quickly, it was as if she were floating across the ground. She completely disappeared into the woods, filled with joy. You can just imagine how happy she was after being healed by Jesus. My faith grew tremendously after this experience. I truly believed that God could heal any disease and any person.

This was the first miracle I personally experienced through the laying on of hands. Before this, I had prayed for people who had headaches, and I had seen someone healed from knee pain during a Bible study. But this was the first miracle I directly took part in. Glory to God—He is the healer, not man.

This encounter completely changed my outlook on who Jesus is and what we are meant to do as His disciples and as His church. I was filled with joy. Since this miraculous encounter, the Lord has continued to use me in this way. I once prayed for an elderly woman in a church where I was invited to preach, and Jesus literally gave her a new heart. She said that while she was lying on the floor being healed, Jesus appeared to her—and she began to cry.

CHAPTER 7

The Horrible Car Accident That Nearly Ended My Life

This is by far the hardest part of the book for me to talk about. It was a dark, rainy Saturday night in the fall. I was on my way to pick up my wife-to-be from work. It was around 10:20 PM when I left home, driving toward Interstate 495. It had just started to rain, and oil was rising from the road surface, making it extremely slippery. The traffic light turned red, and I came to a stop along with three other cars—two in front of me and one on my left.

As my vehicle stopped at the red light, I heard a horrendous screeching of tires behind me. I quickly looked in my rearview mirror and yelled out, "God!"

A white Lincoln Navigator truck, going about 70 mph, hit the far-right corner of the rear bumper of my small Nissan Sentra compact car.

The impact was so severe that it spun my car around in a fraction of a second. I ended up locked bumper-to-bumper with the truck, now facing it—my car had done a complete 180-degree turn.

I do not remember if I was knocked out for a few seconds or minutes. I looked on my right passenger-side, and miraculously, there was a piece of paper and a pen on it. I quickly grabbed the pen and paper as the truck was backing up—fleeing, and unlocking its bumper from mine. I managed to write down the tag number.

The truck drove around us, jumped the curb, and sped away. I opened the door to my car, and a plainclothes police officer approached and asked if I was okay. I replied, "I think so," and handed him the paper with the tag number. He told me to wait on the curb for the ambulance while he chased after the fleeing Lincoln Navigator.

The ambulance arrived and took me to the emergency room. They performed a CAT scan of my brain and body. By the grace of God, nothing had happened to my brain. My body, however, was a different story.

I had six dislocated discs in my back, and every joint in my body was out of place—including my wrists and ankles. I felt lightheaded for several days after the accident. I didn't get into a vehicle for nearly a month due to the trauma it caused me.

Some time later, I was riding in the back seat of a friend's car when I suddenly had a panic attack. I told him to pull over at once.

I got out of the car as fast as possible. My heart was beating fast. After about five minutes, I regained my composure and got back in the car. My friend then drove me home.

The beginning of the horrible pain and the medical treatment

The pain started to show up after the first day, including severe muscle spasms. I could not bend over to touch my toes because of the pain and stiffness. I was going to physical therapy three days per week and to the chiropractor the other two days. I was at the doctor every weekday for an extremely lengthy period of three years.

If you have ever felt low or defeated from suffering pain or difficult situations, take a minute and imagine being at doctors' appointments everyday Monday through Friday, for three straight years. If you are healthy, consider yourself very blessed and thank God every day. Health is one of the greatest blessings a person can have. Take diligent care of your physical, spiritual, and mental wellbeing and you will find balance and health in your life.

The small fiber neuropathy pain I suffered grew stronger after the accident. Before the accident, I had been on a medication that was 80% effective and non-narcotic.

After the accident, that medication could no longer suppress the neuropathic pain. That's when they put me on opioid narcotic painkillers. I was in so much pain that by the time the dosages reached their maximum, I was taking 320 mg a day—enough opioids to knock out a horse.

I was so heavily medicated that I slept anywhere from 12 to 16 hours per day. This went on for a long while.

In addition to the opioids, two spinal cord stimulators were implanted in my back because the medication alone wasn't enough to kill the pain. The surgery was performed before I reached the 320 mg dosage level. Pain from the five 3-inch incisions in my back increased the neuropathic pain even more. The operation lasted two and a half hours and cost nearly a quarter of a million dollars.

It is a good thing that I had insurance to cover the cost. The surgeon told me that I would recover from the incisional pain on my back within 4 to 6 weeks (about 1 and a half months). In reality, it took up to nine months for the back pain to subside somewhat—with the help of both the opioids and the stimulators.

The pain that remained in my back was horrible. I spent most of my days lying in bed. I couldn't sit for more than 10 minutes before the pain became intolerable. Standing was even worse. I could only stand for about five minutes before the pain became unendurable, then I had to lie down to recover.

Eventually, I found another pain specialist who saved my life. He told me that the amount of medication I had been prescribed was enough to kill me. He was amazed that I was even still coherent under such a high dose. When he told me this, I was speechless. Then the doctor recommended another pain killer—one that was far less dangerous and had less milligrams. I am very thankful for this doctor. He has truly been a real blessing in my life. I believe God used him to save my life.

Since the accident, I've also undergone fourteen operative nerve ablations. In a nerve ablation, the doctor makes a small incision, inserts a thin tube into the back to reach the affected nerve, then inserts a laser rod to burn the nerve ending and deaden the pain.

This procedure helped me tremendously. The only downside is that its effects only last for about a year to a year and a half, after which I needed to have it done again.

It has now been 17 years since the accident. Most of that time was spent lying in bed—praying and listening to thousands of hours of sermons by generals of the Christian faith. I calculated that I listened to about **38,400 hours**—or approximately four and a half years' worth—of teaching from the great preachers and evangelists of our time and before.

I used that time wisely. I read Scripture, I listened to countless hours of Bible teachings, I prayed constantly, and prayed in tongues. If it had not been for the power and love of God upholding me every second of every minute, I do not think I could have endured it. I tear up every time I remember how God was so close to me during this time of grief.

I had friends and family that also helped me in those dreadful long years of recovery. Their love and care played a huge role in my recovery. My wife was there for me the whole time. My mom and dad also gave me the moral support that I needed. That support was priceless. I cannot imagine going through this without my wife, the love of my parents, the strength of my church family, and the peace of God.

My bride to be

The accident happened in late October 2008. The following year, in early February, a miracle was about to happen.

I was bombarded with negative thoughts, telling me that my wife would not marry me because I was partially handicapped. But those thoughts were all lies from hell.

I prayed to God for hours, asking him to touch my wife's heart so she would say yes when I proposed to her. Only three weeks after my accident, I finally gathered the courage to ask her to marry me.

We had talked about marriage before the accident, and she had said yes. To my amazement, when I asked her again after the accident, she still said yes. Tears began to run down my face. I was so overwhelmed with joy when she agreed. I felt the love of God pour over me like a waterfall as I hugged her.

I am so happy that God gave me someone with that much love and compassion—to endure over a decade and a half of rehabilitation. She is a true woman of God, and I am truly blessed to have her as my wife.

I cannot stress enough how vital a close relationship with God through prayer has been in surviving the extremely long recovery that I am still in.

CHAPTER 8

Living With Pain For 16 Years

My walk with God has been key to my ongoing recovery. Although I am much better now than I was 16 years ago when the accident occurred, I am still not 100% recovered. My muscles are weak, and I need weight training to regain the strength I lost from the impact. Weight training will be another necessary step toward full recovery. I have faith that by the end of this process, I will be physically stronger than I was 16 years ago.

Going to church and staying faithful to God

During my time of recovery, I always went to church. There were some days when I was in too much pain and couldn't even get out of bed. On those days when I couldn't attend church, I would read my Bible, meditate on the Word, and pray. Congregating with others in church was another important key to my gradual recovery.

Being around Spirit-filled people is essential to any recovery. Nobody needs a room full of negative people bringing them down. You need faith-filled people who know how to pray in order to reach full recovery. Pain is already hard enough to deal with.

The atmosphere you create or allow will affect your spiritual balance and communion with God. I have two choices: I can either surround myself with people who believe in God, or I can sabotage myself by allowing people around me who speak doubt, fear, and defeat.

Negativity is one of the worst spirits anyone can have around them during recovery. It slowly drains the Holy Spirit from the faith-filled person. It does not matter how strong you think you are spiritually—if you fill your environment with doubt and negativity, you are setting yourself up for defeat.

Please choose your environment and the people you allow around you carefully. Choose those who will lift you up and encourage you, not drag you down with pessimism.

Eventually, doubt and disbelief will begin to smother your faith and your belief in your healing—and in God's Word. If our enemy, the devil, is allowed into our personal space, he will slowly dismantle everything God is trying to construct.

Reading God's Word builds and increases our faith. The enemy's plan is to place as many disbelievers as possible into your life to drown out the positive flow of the Holy Spirit. This is one of his favorite strategies.

I could never have spiritually matured if I had remained in the company of my worldly friends after receiving Jesus into my heart. Light and darkness have nothing in common—they are completely opposed to each other and cannot live in communion. God is light and truth; there is no darkness or doubt in Him.

Consider this comparison: someone who is a car mechanic cannot show you how to transplant a heart in a human being. The car mechanic is limited in his knowledge of human anatomy and the complexity of a heart transplant.

So how can someone who does not know God show me the meaning of Scripture or how to hear God's voice and be directed into His will for my life? How can I seek counseling or advice from someone who knows nothing about spiritual realities? Do not let anyone speak into your life if they are filled with a spirit of fear and doubt.

2 Timothy 1:7 says, *"God has not given us a spirit of fear, but of power, love, and a sound mind."*

My point is this: a person cannot grow spiritually or find God's will through the light of His teachings if they seek instruction from someone who is spiritually unlearned and lacks the Holy Spirit. God's instruction never fails; man's often does.

Psalm 32:8 says, *"I will instruct you and teach you the way you should go; I will counsel you with My eye upon you."*

Truth comes through the Spirit of truth—the Holy Spirit of God. When I was younger and less wise, I took advice from worldly people. Not all of it was bad, but it was not God's will and had little to do with the specific and personal journey God had already planned for me.

Some people go to counseling for years, sitting in front of a spiritually unlearned counselor. But how can God's truth come from someone spiritually dead? It cannot. That person will never be able to give you God's solid, holy, unblemished truth. What you will receive is just advice.

1 John 2:27 reminds us that the anointing we have received abides in us, and we do not need anyone to teach us.

Mathew 6:24-26 also teaches us that no man can serve two masters; he will either hate the one and love the other, or be devoted to one and despise the other."

You cannot falter between two opinions and expect to hear clear truth directly from God's lips to your ears. This is the beauty of knowing Jesus. God is omniscient. There is no higher truth than the truth that comes from God's Spirit—there never was, and there never will be.

John 16:13 says, *"When the Spirit of truth comes, He will guide you into all truth."* When we receive Jesus as Savior, we also receive the Holy Spirit.

Staying the course to find your destiny.

Suppose there is a captain who is charting his course. If he marks just one degree off course from his intended destination, that one-degree deviation may seem minor at first. However, the longer you travel on that path, the farther away you'll be from where you were meant to go.

It only takes one degree of deviation on the map to miss a determined destination by a long way.

One word of bad advice, false information, or wrong direction can change the destiny of a person's life. We must be incredibly careful about who we allow to speak into our lives. Please do not take advice from unholy people who do not know or believe in God. I assure you, if you listen to people who do not have the Holy Spirit guiding and speaking through them, you will never receive God's truth—because they are not qualified to speak for God.

The bible says in John 16: 13-15, that the Holy Spirit will guide us into all truth. True and correct advice comes from knowing

God personally. Treat God as if you are speaking to your best friend—because He truly is.

John 15:15 says the following, *"I no longer call you servants, because a servant does not know what his lord does. Instead, I have called you friends, for all things that I have heard from My Father I have made known to you."*

I have learned over the years that Jehovah God is the only one truly qualified to chart the course of my life. When someone gives me advice, I always take it to God in prayer. One misguided word of mistaken advice could cause my life to take an abrupt turn away from God's will.

I cannot stress this enough: it is extremely important to seek advice from Godly people who have Jesus in their hearts and experience in counseling.

This kind of godly counsel will put you on course to victory. Alongside that, we must pursue a personal relationship with God through complete separation from sin and through consistent prayer. Don't invest time in anything that leads you away from your God-given goals and destiny.

Talking to God in prayer—and listening for His response—is a necessary discipline that leads us to His perfect will for our lives. Remember, God's plan is one of prosperity and victory.

3 John 1:2 reads, *"Beloved, I wish above all things that you may prosper and be in health, even as your soul prospers."*

This simply means that as we grow spiritually and mature in our faith, we will also prosper and live in health.

Choosing the right counselor

Choose a counselor who is guided by the Holy Spirit, rather than someone who is not. It is vital to seek a counselor who is a Christian and has a proven record of helping people conquer and resolve their problems.

I went to a counselor after finding out about my dad's infidelity to my mother when I was 13 years old. He was not a born-again believer. However, he did give me some sound advice. He told me to stay away from people who did not have goals—which was excellent advice. He also recommended that I ignore my parents when they argued and not blame myself for their problems. He encouraged me to avoid people with addictions, including alcohol.

He also told me to continue my education, eat well, and stay healthy through weight training and walking.

The advice I received was good and extremely helpful in planning my life. I learned a lot from this doctor during the time I was counseled by him. It was all high-quality advice and seemed to be an excellent foundation to build upon.

However, there was one major piece of the puzzle missing—the most important one. This first step is essential to emotional and spiritual healing and strength.

That first step is to repent and ask for forgiveness of your sins. Ask Jesus to cleanse and forgive you, then invite Him to live in your heart.

Without this crucial first step—having God as your guide—we will be misled, sometimes severely and even permanently.

Jeremiah 33:3 says, *"Call to Me and I will answer you, and show you great and mighty things, which you do not know."*

Jeremiah 29:11 says, *"For I know the plans I have for you, declares the Lord, plans to prosper you and not to harm you, plans to give you a hope and a future."*

The root and foundation must be God. If not, we are building our healing plan from the roof down—completely backward.

God is our source. The seed is the Word of God. Our roots grow deeper as we study and spend time with Him. This practice produces a strong tree of faith, which brings forth good fruit.

How much we grow is directly connected to how much time we spend talking to God in prayer, congregating with other believers, and studying His Word.

The more time we spend with God, the stronger our spirit becomes. And the stronger our spirit, the wiser and more effective we are against the devil and his schemes. In doing so, we can stand firm against all of Satan's attacks and plans.

Life is a battle for everyone, and in this battle, we need the host of angel armies—Jesus Christ—at the wheel of our journey. Jesus has never lost a battle. It is essential to have Him at the center of our lives to overcome every obstacle and storm. He will fight for us and turn favor in our direction.

We must remain connected to Jesus, who is the vine, if we want to be victorious and fulfill the plans God has for us.

John 15:5 says, *"Apart from Me, you can do nothing."*

God adores all of humanity. This is why He gave his only Son as a living sacrifice—so we could be cleansed and forgiven of all our sins. *(Read John 3:16.)*

When we invite Jesus into our hearts, He cleanses us and rebuilds us from the inside out. The old man is renewed, and old, negative thoughts are cast away. We are freed from bondage, fear, and insecurity. Once God enters our hearts to dwell with us, He removes old habits, anger, resentment, and unforgiveness— and grows within us a transformed, improved person, renewed through the Holy Spirit and the hearing of His Word.

The new man in Christ is more powerful, wiser, and victorious than the old one.

Back to the topic of counseling: I was truly fortunate because my counselor was a friend of my mom and dad's. That made it easier for me to open up, unlike speaking to a total stranger. I viewed him like a father figure—except with the training and insight of a doctor. He was extremely helpful in my recovery journey and gave me many tools to help forge a victorious path for my life and make sound decisions.

However, the most important part of that recovery and healing plan was accepting Jesus into my heart as my Lord and Savior. Without that vital decision, I was merely being emotionally pacified and medicated.

Doctors and counselors address the mind, body, and emotions. They may provide medicine and therapeutic tools to help with balance and clarity. But that leaves out the spiritual part of man. We are spirit, soul, and body.

The spiritual aspect of man can only be addressed by somebody who is qualified in the things of the spirit. The physical part must be taken care of, as well as the mind's psychological balance.

The spirit needs to be addressed by a person who has the Holy Spirit and is an experienced counselor or minister.

When I accepted Jesus as my Savior at age 25, I was delivered through prayer by two ministers and a pastor from the demons of depression and alcohol that had bound me.

No amount of counseling could have cast out those demons. I was spiritually bound until those deliverances took place. Demons are clever and skilled at hiding; they cannot be detected by natural means.

True deliverance must come through a Spirit-filled believer who walks upright with God and is anointed for this kind of ministry. I repeat this intentionally, because it is essential for full healing.

In closing this chapter, I want to clearly emphasize: in addition to professional counseling and sound advice, complete healing requires spiritual deliverance—through prayer, by someone who is born again, filled with the Holy Spirit, and experienced in casting out evil spirits.

We cannot ignore the spiritual dimension of recovery if we want full freedom and healing from the spirits sent to oppress us.

The Bible confirms the reality of spiritual infirmity in **Luke 13:11**, where Jesus heals a woman bound by a "spirit of infirmity."

This proves that behind some sickness and suffering, there are indeed spiritual forces at work.

How I viewed success before I accepted Jesus and how I view success now.

I used to view success the way many people still do. It was a very generic point of view. I believed that if I had a good education, it would lead to a good career with a stable income. These factors, in turn, would help me find a good wife and start a family. These are all important things; however, the secular world teaches that these things are the top priority—when in fact, they are not.

Yes, a good education can lead to a good career, but it is not a guaranteed path to true success. This is a worldview the world has adopted—one that often omits any mention of knowing God. It is based on secular knowledge, which has its limits.

If you do not have a personal relationship with Jesus Christ, you could have a doctorate degree and an excellent job and still miss your God-given purpose. I have learned this through personal experience: God's perfect plan for my life far surpasses any idea or plan I could ever come up with.

God has a perfect plan for each one of us. The only way to access that plan—established before the foundations of the earth— is by entering into a personal relationship with Him.

Jeremiah 1:5 says, *"Before I formed you in the womb I knew you, and before you were born I sanctified you."*

God's love and the guidance of the Holy Spirit are perfect. And within that perfection, He has a specific, victorious plan for every person. Asking Jesus to forgive our sins and inviting Him into our hearts as Savior is the only way we will be able to hear God's voice clearly.

John 3:3 says, *"Verily I say unto you, no one can see the kingdom of God unless they are born again."*

Being born again simply means asking Jesus to forgive you of your sins, to cleanse you, and to come into your heart and live there. This relationship grants you access to hear God's voice and to walk in an intimate, personal connection with Him.

In this relationship, God will guide you into His perfect and victorious plan for your life. As a perfect Father, God gives His children only the best. He will never give His children second best or a plan that is destined to fail.

Matthew 7:11 says, *"If you then, being evil, know how to give good gifts to your children, how much more will your Father in heaven give good things to those who ask Him?"*

1 John 1:5 reads, *"God is light, and in Him there is no darkness at all."*

If someone is walking in darkness, they are in danger of stumbling. People who are misled or spiritually unlearned are walking in darkness.

But the path of God is filled with truth and light. Where there is light, a person can see clearly, avoid pitfalls, and make wiser decisions.

AFTERWORD

The purpose of authoring this book is to reach people who are experiencing trauma, depression, low self-esteem, illness, or feelings of brokenness from painful events in their lives. My goal is to tell them that there is a real solution—one that can bring deliverance and healing to the body, soul, and spirit.

Through my personal experience with long-term suffering from small fiber neuropathy, depression, and childhood trauma—and after many years of searching, attending church, counseling, and applying tools that brought physical, emotional, and spiritual healing—I discovered real solutions to these ailments.

I once believed the false notion that people suffering from depression and neuropathy had no options besides lifelong counseling and prescription medications. But I thank God a million times that there is, in fact, a true solution to these conditions and traumas.

Today, I am completely healed from small fiber neuropathy, trauma, drug addiction, and depression—thanks to the steps I discovered through trial and error. These steps, which led to my miraculous healing, are the very ones I've shared within the pages of this book.

I pray that the decades of suffering I endured will serve as a testimony to others—that God is real, that He loves you deeply, and that He will heal anyone who accepts Jesus Christ as Lord and Savior.

To receive the miraculous healing I experienced—healing that only God can provide—we **must** invite Jesus Christ, the Healer, into our hearts. In doing so, you will not only receive the healing you've been longing for, but also salvation and God's perfect plan for your life through a personal relationship with Him.

There was a time I believed I would never get anywhere in life due to the constant pain and afflictions that haunted me daily.

But today, I can proudly and honestly say that I have found true healing for my body, soul, and spirit. I now have the honor of serving as an ordained Minister and Evangelist. I love to pray for those who are physically and mentally oppressed, and I have witnessed God's healing in the lives of many people.

I have a beautiful wife whom I love dearly and an awesome son. I went from the depths of sickness, addiction, and trauma to a life filled with health, purpose, and the love of a wonderful family that I also love dearly.

This is the true story of a young man who was once severely afflicted by trauma, small fiber neuropathy, depression, and drug addiction—but who found healing and deliverance through prayer, studying the Bible, fellowshipping at church, faith, and a personal relationship with Jesus Christ.

ACKNOWLEDGEMENTS

I am eternally grateful to my Lord and Savior, Jesus Christ. If it were not for the strength He gave me, and the healing He provided, I would never have been able to endure the pain I faced daily. Trauma and depression are nearly impossible to overcome without the miraculous help of Jesus. Without His intervention, I would not be completely healed as I am today.

To my beloved wife—thank you for standing by me while I was bedridden after being struck by a drunk driver. You endured so much because of your love for me and your growing faith in God. I'll never forget the countless times you massaged me just so the pain would ease enough for me to sleep. That is real love. Real love suffers and sacrifices for a greater purpose—God's purpose.

To my stepson, who had to witness me lying in bed, in pain, unable to fight for myself: every time you walked through the door after work, my hope and purpose in life were rekindled. I knew I had to stay strong for you and your mother. You gave me a reason to keep going and brought new meaning to the word "family." You are a bright, healthy, positive, and talented young man who loves your mother, me, your work, and playing soccer. I could not have asked for a better son.

I also give thanks to God for bringing my mom and dad to salvation through His dear Son, Jesus. They supported me not only morally but emotionally and spiritually. They visited me at the hospital after my spinal cord stimulator implant surgery, offering their presence, prayers, and comforting home-cooked meals during my long recovery. I miss them dearly, as God has since called them both home to paradise—the final stop before entering heaven.

The love of God and the love of family were instrumental in my 16-year-long battle toward recovery. Those were incredibly difficult years, filled with physical, mental, and spiritual pain that stole a significant portion of my life. But God gave me a loving, caring family—and without them, I cannot imagine having endured this journey or emerging healed as I am today.

I would like to thank Eddie Egesi for the detailed and high-quality work he did in guiding me through the self-publishing process—from designing the cover to ensuring the book was produced to a professional standard. He is easy to work with, kind, and pays close attention to detail. He is also perceptive and offers expert advice across the many skill sets he has been blessed with. I highly recommend checking out his services at apricotbranding.com.

ABOUT THE AUTHOR

Rev. Carlos Leiva is a minister and evangelist with a healing and miracle ministry in the Washington, DC Metropolitan (DMV) area.

Rev. Leiva is fluent in both English and Spanish and has faithfully served the community for over two decades—praying for the sick, preaching the Gospel, offering spiritual counseling, and helping the less fortunate.

He is especially passionate about praying for those afflicted with infirmities and those bound by depression, drug addiction, or other forms of bondage. He finds deep fulfillment in witnessing God break sickness and strongholds through a lifestyle of dedicated prayer and fasting.

If you would like to invite Rev. Carlos Leiva to your church to preach and minister healing, you can contact him at:

revleiva777@gmail.com.

Into The Light Ministry

Intothelightministry.us

www.ingramcontent.com/pod-product-compliance
Lightning Source LLC
Chambersburg PA
CBHW031229120626
46545CB00003B/1045